STOP ARGUING
And Start Talking

Even if you are afraid
your only answer is divorce!

The Secrets of Happy Relationships Series

DR. LAURIE WEISS

Empowerment Systems Books

Stop Arguing and Start Talking...
Even if you are afraid your only answer is divorce!
The Secrets of Happy Relationships Series
Dr. Laurie Weiss
© 2019 Laurie Weiss

All rights reserved. No part of this book may be reproduced in any form or by any electronic or mechanical means, including information storage and retrieval systems, without permission in writing from the publisher, except by a reviewer who may quote brief passages in a review.

The author has done her best to present accurate and up-to-date information in this book, but she cannot guarantee that the information is correct or will suit your particular situation.

This book is sold with the understanding that the publisher and the author are not engaged in rendering any legal, medical, or any other professional services. If expert assistance is required, the services of a competent professional should be sought.

Library of Congress Control Number: 2018913555
Paperback 978-1-949400-16-8
Ebook 978-1-949400-15-1
Downloadable audio file 978-1-949400-17-5

Books may be purchased in quantity by contacting the publisher directly at:

Empowerment Systems Books
506 West Davies Way
Littleton, CO 80120 USA
Phone 303.794.5379
LaurieWeiss@EmpowermentSystems.com
www.EmpowermentSystems.com

Cover: Nick Zelinger, www.NZGraphics.com
Interior Design: Istvan Szabo, Ifj.
Family & Relationships / Marriage & Long-Term Relationships / Self-Help

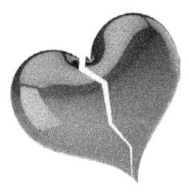

Special Bonus

How to Show Respect—Unconditionally

- What does it really mean to treat someone you love with respect?

- Do you think you are doing so but your loved one disagrees?

- Do you feel that someone doesn't respect you?

- This brief report unravels the mystery you need to understand in order to create the respectful, happy relationship you really want.

Get it now. www.BooksByLaurie.com/respect

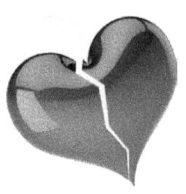

Contents

Special Bonus 3

Chapter 1: When You Don't Agree 6

Chapter 2: He Dragged Me to Counseling 10

Chapter 3: She Tried to Be a Good Wife 14

Chapter 4: Most Unhappy Couples Make These Mistakes 18

Chapter 5: Really Listening 22

Chapter 6: He Thought He Was A Model Husband 25

Chapter 7: They Thought It Was an Argument About Money 30

Chapter 8: Is He Trying to Control You? 34

Chapter 9 Avoid the Circular-Argument Trap—1 39

Chapter 10: Avoid the Circular-Argument Trap—2 42

Chapter 11: Confront the Confusion to Avoid the Fight 48

Chapter 12: Asking Instead of Manipulating 55

Chapter 13: Managing Broken Agreements 58

Chapter 14: How to Get Your 'Honey Do' List Done 62

Chapter 15: Couple's Communication Counseling Verbatim 66

Chapter 16: How to Apologize Even When You Didn't Mean to Cause a Problem 74

Chapter 17: What Do You Say When the Answer Is No? 81

Chapter 18: Conversations Build Happy Relationships 86

Special Bonus Reminder 91

Please Help Me Reach New Readers 93

About the Author 96

How to Work With Dr. Laurie 99

About the Secrets of Happy Relationships Series 103

Books in the Secrets of Happy Relationships Series 106

Other Books by Laurie Weiss 108

Being Happy Together: What to Do to Keep Love Alive 110

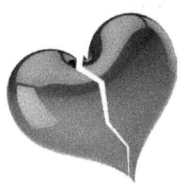

Chapter 1: When You Don't Agree

Does this sound like you?

This was overheard in the dressing room after aerobics class.

Woman One: After all that hassle about getting a new camping trailer we went on the shakedown trip and my husband says he doesn't really enjoy camping anymore. I told him in the beginning that I thought it was a mistake, but he wouldn't listen. I am so disgusted...

Woman Two: I'm glad I don't have a husband like that.

Stop Arguing and Start Talking

Woman One: I wish I didn't.

Or would you be a part of this conversation?

This is a new couple at their first counseling session. They are telling me why they have come.

He: She could have told me she was going to leave. After all we've been together for seven years, and she'd knows I don't mean it when I yell. I'm just letting off steam and then I calm down. I didn't think she really meant for me to stop. I miss her so much, and I miss the kids. What can I do to get her to change her mind?

She: I want to come back, but he just doesn't get it. The yelling scares me and the kids and all he cares about is having me in bed. He loves the kids, but I did tell him that if he didn't change, I would leave. I told him at least 10 times. That that just shows how much he listens to me.

No, I don't have another man in my life. At this point it's tough just to live. This cramped apartment is all I can afford, and it's tough be a single mom. But I don't think he can really change.

He: I know I can change—you've got to give me a chance. Just tell me what you want me to do and I'll do it. Just tell me!

She: I want you to think about what I say. I just told you again what I want—but did you listen? No! Just quit yelling at me and talk to me like a person.

He: I just yell for a minute when I get upset. The kids get over it. And it shouldn't bother you so much.

Me: But it does upset her. Imagine what it's like from her point of view. Have you ever been yelled at?

He: She yells all the time. I can't do anything right. There's no way to please her. She yells just like my mom did when I was a kid.

Me: What does she yell about?

She: I just asked him to pick up the stuff he leaves around. Sometimes it's tough, with his dishes in the sink and wanting him to help me with the kids' baths. I need to be louder because he can't hear me over the TV, but he doesn't listen anyway.

Stop Arguing and Start Talking

He: I help—you're just never satisfied.

Me: Slow down! I want you to try something different. Do you really want this marriage to work?

Chapter 2:
He Dragged Me to Counseling

There's no way to know ahead of time exactly what your marriage is going to be like. I certainly didn't know for mine. For the first few years my learning came from experience.

I don't know whether my husband suspected something was wrong before I did, or whether he took me to a therapist simply because he was in graduate school learning how to be a therapist himself. We had been married for a couple of years—long enough for the honeymoon to definitely be over.

Stop Arguing and Start Talking

What I remember most vividly from that first session was confessing one of my shortcomings—about not really being excited by music my husband loved. What the therapist said was a revelation. He told me it was okay for me to continue to love Opera even though my husband loved jazz. Until that moment both Jonathan and I believed that it was my job to give up what I loved and embrace what he loved in every area of our lives.

I wish I'd known that you don't have to give up yourself to be in a marriage.

By trying to turn myself into that mythological one I was supposed to become after we got married, I had assumed that I had to give up anything about myself that he didn't like and that in exchange he was supposed to fulfill all my emotional needs. Women have progressed since then but not as much as I wish we had.

Even now, some women still try to shut down important parts of themselves to merge with their partners. That didn't work in 1960 and it doesn't work now.

I assumed my marriage would be traditional, a lot like my mother's. I thought that my purpose in life was to be a wife and mother. I assumed that I would be responsible for the household, for the grocery shopping and for the childcare. I also assumed that he would be the sole wage earner in the family.

My husband shared some of those assumptions. But there were two problems. One, I didn't know which assumptions he shared, and two, I was working outside the home to support us while he attended school.

I assumed that I was the only responsible person in the world. I was angry at him without really knowing that I was angry. Actually, after a while, I was angry in general at my life but not aware that I had any other options. I had no clue that my hidden emotions impacted my behavior, but I'll bet it has something to do with the reason my husband suggested that we see that wonderful therapist who helped me begin to wake up.

You may be avoiding doing something important because it would mean taking a risk. And the possibility of failure seems overwhelmingly scary. You may have little confidence that counseling could work for your situation, but you may be underestimating yourself.

It takes time and work to dismantle your automatic pilot and live your life the way you choose to live it. Even when you do, the automatic pilot still shows up and tries to take over when you're not paying attention.

After nearly 60 years of marriage, at least 50 of them spent consciously learning and growing, I still find myself slipping back into some of the traditional, comfortable patterns I thought I had given up long ago. Instead of fighting them the way I used to, I try to ask myself what purpose they are serving in my life and then decide whether or not to keep them.

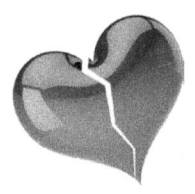

Chapter 3:
She Tried to Be a Good Wife

How do I move from "one-down" to equal?

How can I make my husband always be happy with me?

How can I find love with my partner again?

These are related questions. Any one of them could have been asked by May, who has been married for only three years. It's the same story I have heard from dozens of women over the years.

It's my story, too. I keep thinking that the world has changed a lot since I was newly married in 1960. Yet the old myths about how to create a marriage haven't died yet and still cause incredible unhappiness.

This conversation I had with May is quite similar to my first conversation with my marriage counselor when I had been married just a short time.

May: I don't know what's wrong. I feel so miserable. For months I did everything I knew how to do to be a good wife and please him. Even though we both work I decided it was my job to make sure we eat well so I came home and made dinner. I did things he wanted to do.

I feel more and more alone and can barely make myself do those things anymore. I really think I need to leave him to find myself again. But I really do want to make this marriage work.

Dr. Laurie: Have you talked to him about how you feel?

May: I'm too embarrassed. I hardly want to talk to him at all. When I do talk to him, he just tries to fix it and that's even worse. I wish he just listened to me.

Dr. Laurie: It sounds like he thinks it's his job to fix any problem that you tell him about. Have you ever told him what you do want him to do?

May: Not really—I guess we really don't talk much about stuff like this at all.

Dr. Laurie: It sounds as if each of you is doing what you think you're supposed to do to make this marriage work—and it's not working. How did you learn about what you're supposed to do to be a good wife?

May: Well my mom always put my dad first and told us kids to do so also. I just thought that's the way you're supposed to do it.

Dr. Laurie: The truth is that there isn't any "supposed to" in marriage or any other relationship. It's important to learn to talk to each other about what's most important to each of you.

The problem is that most of the old rules say, "don't talk about it, just do it." I think relationships work a lot better when you each learn to ask for what you want and to negotiate when what you want doesn't match what your partner wants.

These are skills that take a while to develop. It's worth learning how to practice them. I have lots of tools that will help. Is your husband willing to work with you on this?

May: I'm pretty sure he is. We've been talking about whether we can make this work and I know he wants to also.

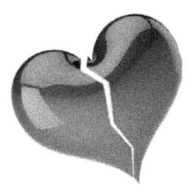

Chapter 4: Most Unhappy Couples Make These Mistakes

In the more than 45 years I have worked with unhappy couples I am always amazed at how many of them conclude that they must have made a mistake and chosen the wrong partner. They think the solution is to find a new partner and hope they'll make a better choice the next time.

Nothing could be further from the truth!

I am always sad when I hear about couples that separate just because they don't understand what is causing their unhappiness. It is just such an unnecessary waste.

If you want to give your relationship a fair chance to really succeed and give you the joy you want and deserve, here is what you must know about the most catastrophic mistakes that unhappy couples make.

Mistake #1. Trying to keep the relationship from changing.

Most relationships start with an intense romance. It's exciting and fun and consuming. It's nature's way of ensuring the survival of the race by drawing people together long enough for them to make babies. However, it is only temporary! A healthy relationship will grow and change, and the intensity can grow into a deeper and more sustaining love—if you don't try to keep it from changing.

Mistake #2. Expecting your partner to read your mind—to know what you want and give it to you automatically.

Mind reading is a very inexact science. Your partner isn't necessarily doing something wrong or neglecting his or her duty to you. S/he is simply incapable of knowing exactly what you want until you explain it clearly. Even then, your partner may be unable or unwilling to give you what you want because of conflicting demands on his or her energy.

You both must learn to negotiate with each other to avoid the unhappiness that comes when you each make this mistake.

Mistake #3. Trying to make two people become one.

If you try to accomplish this impossible task, each person must discard half of his or her self to participate in the relationship. While many people can put aside important parts of themselves for a while and pretend those parts don't exist, it just doesn't work long-term.

The person who loves to be outdoors but gives up hiking to adapt to her partner's preference for movies and sports bars will soon feel unhappy and resentful, destroying the illusion of blissful togetherness.

So, as you struggle to create a happy relationship, chances are you need to correct at least one of these mistakes. The good news is that you can use this information to stop doing what doesn't work and start creating a long-lasting and loving relationship right now.

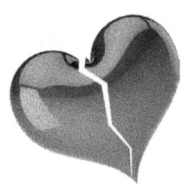

Chapter 5:

Really Listening

Once, my husband and I were asked to appear on the Oprah Winfrey Show. It never happened, but it certainly gave me a lot to think about.

The proposed show topic was non-traditional marriages, and we were invited because of our professional expertise on the subject, as well as our own personal examples. Since we look fairly ordinary on the outside, many of our friends asked, "What is non-traditional about your marriage?"

Lots of things—especially considering where we started from: It took years to move from a very traditional marriage to a marriage with completely shared responsibility for the household, children (until they grew up) and our business. Along the way we argued (frequently), considered divorce (a few times) and supported each other in doing even the things we wished the other wouldn't do at all.

Perhaps the most important, and the most non-traditional part of our marriage are these three commitments:

- to be responsible for communicating what we feel, need and want to each other;
- to *Really Listen* to each other;
- and to support each other's growth, regardless of the perceived risk to ourselves and to the relationship.

Without *Really Listening* to each other, everything else falls apart. It is the basis of all successful relationships. *Really Listening* to another person communicates to them "I know that you exist, and your existence is important to me." It is the fundamental recognition we all need in order to feel that we have value in the world.

It is the response that people are willing to do almost anything to get. It is also the response that is missing in most of the troubled relationships I encounter in my work.

Really Listening means paying attention to another person's words, feelings and meaning, and saying and doing things that let another person know that you truly understand. *Really Listening* means waiting to state your own thoughts until you are certain the other person feels they have been heard and understood.

Really Listening works best when it is bilateral—when the other person listens back. Listening does not necessarily mean agreeing, it means respecting and acknowledging one another.

Really Listening may be the greatest, and least expensive, gift you can give to another person!

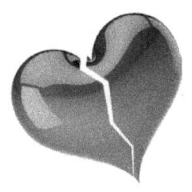

Chapter 6:
He Thought He Was A Model Husband

You may believe that never arguing with each other means your relationship is strong. What usually happens though, is that because you're both human, you have different needs and wants.

If you never even notice, let alone discuss (argue about?) your different needs and wants, you may not even realize the damage you're doing to your relationship.

That's the problem that brought Jeff to my office.

Jeff was stunned when Eileen announced that she wanted a divorce. For nine years he had considered himself a model husband, never arguing, letting her do whatever she wanted to do and working hard to increase his income to support their lifestyle.

He begged her to reconsider and offered to seek counseling to prove he was willing to change. However, he had trouble imagining how he could do anything differently.

Eileen refused to come to counseling with him. Her position was that if he couldn't figure it out for himself, it proved he was hopeless.

As we talked, it was clear that Jeff knew what he liked to do and how he felt about lots of things, but he had very little information about Eileen. He was puzzled about her seemingly odd priorities.

Why would she want to redecorate the living room? It seemed fine to him. Nevertheless, he was fine with her repainting the room and putting in a new floor by herself. He was a little annoyed by the mess and by her being too tired for much lovemaking, but he managed.

He also admitted he was a little annoyed when Eileen attended meetings several nights a week, but he never said anything to her about it. He usually got involved in online computer exchanges with others when she was away; in fact, he got so engrossed that he wouldn't even notice when she came home and went to bed.

Jeff had no idea what her meetings were about. He was surprised when I suggested that he ask her, but he agreed to experiment by doing his best to ask and to *Really Listen* to her answer. To demonstrate to her that he was listening, he was to try to restate what she said.

The next week Jeff reported that Eileen was so encouraged that she was now willing to set up a joint counseling meeting.

Jeff admitted that he wasn't particularly happy in his marriage either but thought that was normal. Growing up with his divorced mother, who did whatever she could to make his life easier, he had never really had the opportunity to see a couple discuss differences or solve problems together.

Eileen was understandably furious at Jeff for ignoring her for so many years. She had made many attempts to tell him about what she needed, but he had never even noticed. Finally, she had started attending a support group and a study group, both of which had helped her decide to leave her joyless marriage.

However, Jeff's recent attempts to listen to her made her hopeful that *he could change.* She was surprised to discover that Jeff had never learned the basic emotional skills that he needed to create a more satisfying relationship.

Learning life skills takes time, and Jeff and Eileen decided to wait six months before deciding about whether to stay together. Jeff participated in a counseling group, and they had couples' sessions at least once a month.

Their marriage did become more satisfying, and they decided to stay together. They stayed in counseling until they mastered the art of supporting each other's growth.

Being happy together in your relationship doesn't necessarily require counseling. There is a lot you can do together to create a conscious, loving and mature life partnership. What you do need is a commitment to having the important conversations that allow you to really know and understand each other.

Many of the other books in *The Secrets of Happy Relationships Series* will help you to learn to have those conversations.

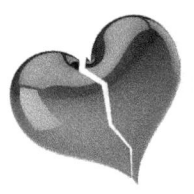

Chapter 7: They Thought It Was an Argument About Money

Five years into his second marriage, Jim was so frustrated with the haphazard way Cathy seemed to handle her finances that he was seriously considering divorce. Cathy wouldn't consider joint counseling, so he hired me to help him sort through the issues and decide what to do.

Jim & Cathy were both well-paid professionals and had a clear agreement to share expenses. Jim believed that Cathy wasn't really keeping the agreement. He gathered evidence to prove his point.

- Cathy kept forgetting her wallet or running short of cash, manipulating him into paying for all their entertainment expenses.

- When he asked her to pay him back, she never seemed to get around to it. He felt ashamed to make an issue of repayment, so he usually let it drop.

- Cathy did pay her share of household bills, but Jim was so worried about her "flakiness" that he frequently questioned her anxiously about whether she was up to date.

- At one point, after hearing her talk about wanting a new car, he carefully researched which new car would be best for her. He was appalled when she bought a more expensive, sportier model.

- He urged her to keep careful records of her personal expenditures and offered to help her review them. She refused angrily, and they had frequent arguments about money.

When I asked Jim what he did to contribute to the problem, Jim recognized that *he was the one who started the arguments* by frequently asking Cathy about what she did with her money. It seemed as if Jim was collecting evidence to support his arguments instead of looking at what was really bothering him.

When I asked what he was trying to accomplish by questioning her, Jim first said he just wanted her to be responsible. When he dug a little deeper, he realized that he wanted to be sure she could take care of herself financially and not become dependent on him.

He also recognized that frequently questioning her was not accomplishing his goal. In fact, it was making the problem even worse.

Jim also discovered that he had mixed feelings about whether a husband should be financially responsible for his wife. This ambivalence kept him from discussing the only real problem—that Cathy was breaking her financial agreement to share entertainment costs.

I asked Jim if his unexpressed resentment about the broken agreement might be connected to his judgment that she was irresponsible about money. He already knew that the "evidence" didn't really support his judgment. Cathy was responsible for everything *except* sharing entertainment expenses. The connection made sense to him.

Jim still didn't feel ready to discuss the broken agreement with Cathy, but he decided to experiment with not asking her about how she managed her own money. He also decided to tell Cathy in advance whether any entertainment activity would be his treat.

A month after he started his experiment, Jim noticed that the arguments had almost completely disappeared. The bills continued to get paid, and Cathy was occasionally volunteering to treat him to dinner and other activities.

He decided to stay married.

It is important to remember that almost everything you do is done for a reason, but sometimes you must look below the surface to discover the important, but hidden, reason for your behavior.

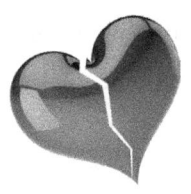

Chapter 8:
Is He Trying to Control You?

"My husband is always telling me what to do. How can I keep living with a person who tries to control everyone?" Gail was so frustrated she was almost in tears.

How often do you fume about someone's attempts to control you? In some relationships it happens way too often for comfort—especially in "co-dependent relationships" where both partners agree that one partner's needs are more important than the needs of the other.

If someone else seems to be controlling your life, try looking at the bigger picture.

- Has someone else managed to control you before?
- Have you had at least one person like this in your life for as long as you can remember?

If you answered yes to either of these questions, it's useful to discover how you are cooperating in maintaining such an unproductive relationship—and to explore your options for changing.

Changing may be a lot easier than you think if you do it in baby steps.

WARNING: If you are in a relationship where you are being physically or emotionally threatened, this will help you change the way you think, but you must still take steps to ensure your own safety. *If you are in danger, your safety must be your first concern.*

First, practice changing the way you talk about your complaints—especially the way you talk to yourself about them. You must learn to stop seeing yourself as a victim.

Your goal here is to see yourself as a fully functional, mature individual who is participating in the discomfort of your relationship.

Since you probably believe that the other person needs to change first, this may be a difficult task. Stick with it. You need to stop blaming anyone else and change your own attitude instead.

Try to recall how you and the controlling person have played out some agreements that you may have never recognized before. These examples may help. You probably won't like the restatement but see if it rings true anyway.

- "My husband rules our house with an iron fist." This could turn into "I have agreed to be ruled by my husband in our marriage. I have done this by doing what he has told me to do (probably) since the beginning of our relationship. I have also taught our children to follow his instructions either directly or by setting an example for them."

- "He makes all the decisions. He tells me what I should do." This could be: "I ask him for his guidance before I choose to do anything. When I want to do something on my own, I ask permission; then when he refuses, I do not do what I would like to do."

- "How can I learn to live with a person like this?" could become: "I choose to live with this man because he provides things for me that I want and need, even though I sometimes resent the cost. I am afraid to stand up for what I want because I feel I'll risk losing the emotional and physical security he has provided for me all these years. I am also not sure I could make it on my own without him. I have very little confidence in my own ability to take care of myself and our children."

Each restatement is another building block to move toward a position of self-responsibility.

You may feel very strange and unfamiliar with this new perspective, but the more often you focus on thinking this way, the more quickly you will learn to reclaim your own power.

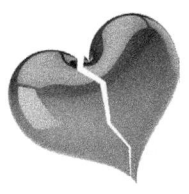

Chapter 9
Avoid the Circular-Argument Trap—1

In all the years I've been helping couples learn to communicate with each other, I'm always amazed at how many of them are frustrated because they can never finish a simple conversation together. In fact, many of them tell me that all conversations end in confusing arguments that only go around in circles.

It doesn't have to be that way. I am sad that so many relationships end in disaster because couples just don't know how to get out of the *Circular-Argument* trap.

If you want to learn to avoid this trap, use these three simple methods to sidestep this challenge. Your conversations really can end with the feeling of completion instead of with an argument.

You may not end up in agreement but at least you will understand each other's positions.

- First, you need to decide why you are having the conversation in the first place. It can even be as simple as wanting to know what time your partner is going to meet you after work. You really *must* start with the end in mind.

- Second, no matter what your partner says about some other topic, you need to respond to his or her new topic *and* also remember why you're having the conversation.

- Your partner may say he will have a busy afternoon because of a big project. First, say "Yes, I know you'll be busy." Then instead of talking about why he's busy, *remember* that you want to set a meeting time. If you forget this step you have already accepted his invitation to get back into the circle trap.

- Third, you must remind your partner about the original reason for your conversation. After sympathizing with your partner about how busy he'll be, REMIND him that all you want to know is what time he can meet you.

Wash, rinse and repeat as necessary.

Some of the couples I've worked with find that they're so addicted to this pattern that it's necessary to come back to the original question several times before it is answered.

It sounds simple, and it is. But it may not be easy. If you are in the habit of just responding to the last thing that was said, you stay trapped in the confusion until you adopt this simple technique. Remember it—the more you practice the easier it will be.

Chapter 10:
Avoid the Circular-Argument Trap—2

Here is another example of how easy it is to get caught in the *Circular-Argument* trap and how to manage to stay out of it.

You've been in this kind of frustrating conversation, too. You know, the kind that seems ok until you are surprised by a problem that you thought was already handled. Then you wonder what happened and why the original problem didn't get solved.

It happens at work. It happens at home. It happens when you're a customer. It happens on a bad tech support call.

Stop Arguing and Start Talking

And most of the time you don't even notice until you're deep into a quagmire.

It starts innocently enough. You have a question or problem that you tell another person. That person picks up a small detail from what you have said and says something about the detail. You, either because you are too polite to point out that your main point was something else, or because you got emotionally involved in the response you heard and didn't notice, unwittingly follow the other person into never-never land.

Instead of going back to your original conversation and your original point as I suggested earlier, you give the socially appropriate and politically correct response. You continue the conversation by talking about what you just heard. You probably don't even notice that your conversation partner has changed the subject.

You may even now be talking about a small detail from what was said to you. You're vulnerable to doing this if the conversation is emotionally loaded or if you have a strong disagreement with one of the details. But it can happen even in very ordinary circumstances. If you do this, the conversation is doomed.

Anything you say in response will lead to another round. Your conversation partner (or opponent) will choose a detail from everything you say and respond to that, possibly with a long and involved emotional story. You in turn respond to a detail from his story and so forth...

It goes something like this.

You: Will you be able to be here when the package arrives this afternoon?

Your Spouse: How come you can't be here to get it? (*Your question hasn't been answered.*)

You: I have a dentist appointment. (*You are still being straightforward and answering a question. You still have a chance to redeem this conversation.*)

Your Spouse: I had a dentist appointment last week. It didn't hurt much except when it came time to pay. (*What does that have to do with being present when the package arrives???)*

You: Didn't you use the dental insurance? (*Now you're lost. You're getting further and further away from finding out whether she/he will be there to receive your package.*)

Your Spouse: Yes, but I've had so much work done they won't cover any more. (*Now what do you do? I'll bet you don't even remember the original conversation.*)

You: Gee, I wonder if I'm close to my limit. I better check. (*Later you go to check your insurance. You find a notice that the package arrived, and no one was there to receive it.*)

And then you remember that you asked him if he would be there to get the package, but you never got an answer.

There is a better way. It involves paying attention and risking being a little bit impolite or politically incorrect. It also avoids problems like needing to have the package redelivered later, as well as many different types of misunderstanding.

Your new conversation might sound like this.

You: Will you be able to be here when the package arrives this afternoon?

Your Spouse: How come you can't be here to get it? (Your question hasn't been answered, but this time you notice.)

You: I have a dentist appointment. (You are still being polite and straightforward, and you have answered the question. You still have a chance to redeem this conversation.)

You: That's why I need to know if you can be here to accept the package when it arrives. (*You are still being polite while going back to your original topic.*)

Your Spouse: You know, I was thinking of going to work out. (*Keep paying attention. This is a choice point. Do you have a conversation about the importance of exercise or do you get your question answered? Now you can risk being a little impolite.*)

You: I know you want to work out, but I still need to know if you will be here this afternoon.

Your Spouse: Well, I was planning on going to the gym. (*That's closer, but you still haven't pinned down an answer.*)

You: Okay I'll leave a note on the door for them to deliver it next door. (*You've solved the problem without a confrontation. You can have the conversation about exercising another time.*)

The second conversation takes attention and some creativity. You need to make deliberate choices about how to respond to indirect communication. The more often you make those choices, the more effective you will be.

Dare to Say It is a special report that explores how to manage this kind of conversation in a business setting. Copies are available at DareToSayIt.com.

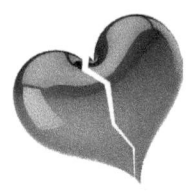

Chapter 11: Confront the Confusion to Avoid the Fight

It's extremely easy to fall into a fight in even the most enlightened relationship. My husband and I *almost* did it recently. In fact, if you had been watching—you might have called our conversation a fight, or at least an argument...

To put this in proper perspective, you should know that this happened when we had been married for 48 years and had been studying and teaching about relationships for over 35 years.

Stop Arguing and Start Talking

It started innocently enough. My husband Jonathan came into my office and started a conversation.

Jonathan: I've been invited to a meeting tonight. I'm going to go. Would you like to come along with me?

Me: Tell me more.

Jonathan: A friend told me he attended "x" workshop and came away feeling less guilty and pressured about getting stuff done. You have been struggling with that, so I thought you might find it useful.

I missed something in this exchange. I've known about "x" workshop for a long time and have never been particularly interested in attending it. His comment was ambiguous, but I thought he was talking about the evening program. In his mind his invitation was about the workshop.

Me: OK, I'll come.

I asked for details, and he gave me a location and starting time. Both were very doable. I asked about the ending time, and he said he didn't know. He called to find out. Later, he told me, "The meeting ends at 10:45. Maybe we should take both cars in case you want to leave early."

Now, I was a little bit unsure about the meeting since I had been out late the night before, but I didn't say anything. A little later, I overheard his end of a telephone conversation with our adult son. He talked about saving the *workshop* dates, because our son might like to attend with us. At this point I was getting a little confused and suspicious.

Me: (later in his office). What is this about? Are you planning to attend the workshop?

Jonathan: Well, my friend told me how much it changed since I was involved years ago.

I was again beginning to feel angry because he didn't actually answer my question.

Me: (impatient) Tell me the whole thing.

Jonathan: I did. I'm thinking about it.

Stop Arguing and Start Talking

Me: (Angrily—this is the part that looked like the fight.) Tell me the whole thing, starting at the beginning.

Jonathan: (defensively). Why are you mad at me? I did tell you.

Me: No you didn't. If you had told me the whole thing, you would have started with telling me that you were thinking about going to the workshop, instead of inviting me to attend the meeting. What is this thing tonight anyway? Is it a preview for the workshop? (We both know that a preview is a sales presentation.)

Jonathan: Well my friend said they don't pressure you anymore. He said they've changed.

Me: (I'm angry -- he has SORT OF admitted that it's a sales presentation.) I thought you said it was about helping me feel less pressured.

Jonathan: (innocent). Why are you so angry?

Me: Because you're not giving me the whole story straight—it's coming out in pieces.

I left his office telling him I would think about it. This brief angry exchange could've turned into an ugly fight. In fact, it had all the earmarks of one of the games described in Eric Berne's classic book *Games People Play*.

It started with an invitation that had an ulterior motive. Jonathan wanted me to do something that he was pretty sure I wouldn't be very interested in doing, so he offered me an ambiguous invitation.

If I had attended the evening meeting and been subjected to a sales presentation instead of getting useful information I expected, I really would have been angry. He really was not thinking about trying to manipulate me at the time he invited me. All he was thinking about was what he wanted to do.

Games start that way and end with everyone involved feeling badly. They can get out of control very quickly. Then it becomes a matter of blaming each other for the problem.

Stop Arguing and Start Talking

If I had gone to the meeting without getting the additional information, I would have been angry. And I certainly could have blamed him for tricking me. Really, though, I would have had a part in being tricked. My part would have been falling for the bait of a pleasant evening out and not noticing that there was something else going on.

That is what would have happened if I hadn't noticed my own confusion after I overheard Jonathan's phone call and started asking questions.

In every game, there's a moment of confusion that is usually ignored. That confusion often involves the start of a Circular-Argument. Once it's ignored, the game or the fight escalates into a mess of bad feelings and accusations.

I've been practicing noticing those moments for many years. Even when I did notice that something else was going on and tried to get more information, I still got angry. But we did manage to avoid a fight.

Later when I had calmed down, I thought about whether I really wanted to attend the meeting. I decided that I didn't want to go and said, "I'll pass." He said OK and went to the meeting while I had a quiet, pleasant evening at home.

Much later, he came home and said, "It's probably a good thing that you didn't go. You wouldn't have liked it."

Me: Are you going to attend the workshop?

Jonathan: I'm thinking about it.

Communication can be a real challenge, even when you are as skilled at it as I was then. It's important to learn to notice those moments of confusion and talk about them. Sometimes that works, and you can avoid getting deeper into an argument.

If it doesn't work—and the fight happens anyway—trying to assign blame won't get you very far. In fact, you may start another fight while trying to sort out the first one. If you can, just forgive each other and move on.

If fights happen frequently, talk to a professional relationship counselor. We can help you learn more effective patterns of communication.

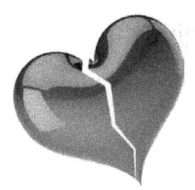

Chapter 12:
Asking Instead of Manipulating

As a woman raised in a traditional family, I didn't know I had the right to ask for what I wanted, if I even knew what it was. Often, I did not even notice what I wanted because I was so intent on pleasing others.

Instead, like many women, when I did want something, I used many strategies to try to get it from my husband without asking for it.

My first strategy was to hint. I would talk about how much I admired something and how nice it would be to have it. If that didn't work I might whine about not having it. Then, I might try giving him what I wanted and hope he would notice and give it back to me.

When we were first in business together, I even tried to drive the business in the direction I thought it should go by pushing Jonathan ahead of me and pretending that he was the leader. That was a really, really bad idea.

You end up doing a lot of unproductive manipulation when you don't know that you have the right to ask for what you want.

However, asking for what you want can seem very risky. It can be embarrassing when you put yourself out there, ask and expose your vulnerability, and have someone refuse your request. That is especially true if you've spent years being a good little girl and were told to be polite in hopes that someone would notice you.

Learning to ask for what you want is the first step of negotiation with someone else. That someone also has desires that may or may not match yours. It is an important first step.

It's also important to recognize that if you don't get what you ask for, you are in essentially the same position you were in before you asked. You didn't have it then and you still don't have it.

You can start learning to ask by asking for small things you don't really need, like having someone bring you a cup of coffee that you could easily get up to get by yourself. Then, as you get more comfortable with the process, you can progress to asking for more important things.

You will eventually discover that you greatly increase the odds of getting what you want when you ask for it directly. You will also discover that being told "no" is not as terrible as you imagined it might be.

Chapter 13:
Managing Broken Agreements

What can you do if someone you love is doing something that's bad for him or bad for you? What if he is breaking agreements that you have made, refusing to acknowledge that there's anything wrong, and then blaming you and telling you that you're crazy for calling the problem to his attention?

Marilyn was faced with just such a dilemma. Six weeks earlier, she and her husband were both delighted that he had completed a major project. The project had kept him too busy to allow him to spend much time at home with her and their two small children for several months. He was planning to take some time to figure out what he really wanted to do with his life and start working toward a career change. They were also looking forward to spending time together to renew their relationship.

Suddenly, without consulting her, he started a second, low-paying, full-time job. He was working 80 hours a week; he had decided that they needed to save more money. He cut her household allowance and her access to emergency money. She felt helpless and victimized!

Fortunately, she was a member of one of our therapy groups at the time. Group members helped her decide that she needed to help her spouse become as uncomfortable with his decisions as she was. They helped her figure out what would make it worth his while to pay attention to her.

She was already refusing to make him lunch or alter her schedule to help him manage his new responsibilities. She discussed and discarded the possibility of getting a new charge card and spending money on things she wanted because of the negative impact on herself and the family. When the other group members suggested she go on strike and not take care of the house, she decided that would be unpleasant for her and the children. She also ruled out refusing sex because she enjoyed it too much.

Finally, Marilyn came up with an extremely creative solution. She brought home a fifteen-pound bag of dry navy beans, showed it to him, and told him that if he didn't listen to her concerns and focus on finding a job that was meaningful and appropriate for him (instead of acting like a workaholic), she would serve him bean soup every night for dinner until he went back to their mutually agreed upon objectives.

At the next group meeting a week later she was ecstatic. He did listen to her. He had already put in several applications for the kind of job he really wanted and agreed to quit his second job within a reasonable period. He also stopped trying to control her access to money for appropriate expenses.

Stop Arguing and Start Talking

The beans are still visible on the kitchen table. He's asked her to put them away, but she says she won't do so until he has completed his part of the agreement about actually spending time with the family.

Back in group, Marilyn reaffirmed her own power to not accept victimhood just because her husband tends toward workaholism. She knows she will have to keep standing up for herself until he decides to examine his own addictive patterns.

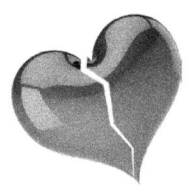

Chapter 14:

How to Get Your

'Honey Do' List Done

Are you a woman who has moments when you sometimes want to murder your loving husband because he agrees to do everything you ask him to do but then never seems to get it done?

It's even more frustrating when you gather your courage to talk to him once more, and he again promises he'll finish the taxes, or fix the leaky faucet, or paint the bathroom, or organize the sports equipment in the garage.

Stop Arguing and Start Talking

And then, again, he has a really good reason why he can't do it when he promised—or he just forgets—or he gets it almost done but leaves one critical piece like doing the final cleanup on a project.

Here is the almost magical secret that will not only get those jobs completed but get you out of the role of nag. And the best part—it doesn't involve doing the job yourself.

By the way, this secret works with kids, committee members and service people as well as husbands. Best of all, you can use it any time during the cycle of "promise to do something, forget, remind, forget, remind, make excuses, remind, etc.!"

It may seem kind of silly or unnecessary, but when you do it, it nearly always works. It does involve some record keeping and being willing to take a firm stand and not cave in.

It might be called a power play on your part, but that's okay—it will be completely on the up and up because you'll tell him in advance exactly what you're going to do.

Next time you're ready to remind him about the undone task, use this process.

1. Ask him for a firm agreement—day and time—when the job will be done.

2. Figure out who else could do the job—a handyman? A tax preparation service? The teenager next door? A plumbing service? Then estimate how much it will cost. Resolve to take the money from a source your husband will notice but won't be too tough on anyone – like your grocery budget—it's okay to serve beans for a week (remember Marilyn) or forego your regular night out to pay to get the task done.

3. Tell him what you plan to do if he doesn't keep his agreement.

4. When the deadline approaches, remind him of your plan.

5. If he misses the deadline, bite the bullet and carry out your plan. Usually, you'll only need to do this once to convince your husband that you expect him to keep his promises.

Of course, this could lead to a discussion of making more realistic agreements or creating a priority list of which things are really important or even a plan about what to keep in-house and what to outsource.

So, gather up your courage and tell him your plan. It's much more effective than the pattern of excuses followed by nagging to get him to keep his promises. Simply follow the steps, and you'll be on your way to creating a new way to solve problems together.

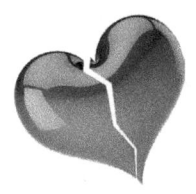

Chapter 15:

Couple's Communication Counseling Verbatim

It's amazing how often conversations between people who truly love each other get totally confused. Most of the couples I work with face this predicament, regardless of what else is going on.

Sometimes they wait a long time to come for counseling, often because one or both of them is scared about what's going to happen in that mysterious place, the counselor's office. You may even be wondering about this yourself.

Stop Arguing and Start Talking

This couple gave me permission to let you know the details of their conversations with me.

He is a respected professional, and she was a stay-at-home mom until recently when she took a part-time job. They have two children, a teenager and a nine-year-old.

Good relationships are built and rebuilt one conversation at a time. This is one of the many conversations we've had, rebuilding their relationship after they came close to ending it.

The Conversation

She: We had another argument. We got through it, but I want to talk about it.

Me: OK, talk to each other.

He: I hate it when you get mad at me at night over little things I don't even remember.

She: Sometimes you do such nasty stuff. It makes me feel like I hate you. Remember, like dumping the neighbor's dog's poop off our lawn and back into their driveway instead of just cleaning it up. When that happens, I wonder why I married you.

He: (with a slight grin) They deserved it.

She: You don't have to do stuff like that.

He: I was teaching him a lesson. He should control his dog.

She: And you do stuff like that with the kids too, and I see people look at me. They wonder why I put up with you.

Me: You don't feel that way all the time, do you?

She: (completely changing her angry position) Oh no, deep down inside I know he is kind and loving and really cares about me. (Smiling) I know that!

Me: But you're really angry about some of his behavior, aren't you?

She: Yeah.

Me: What do you actually do at the time this kind of behavior is happening?

Stop Arguing and Start Talking

She: Sometimes I tell him how stupid he is to do it.

Me: Is that later, at night?

She: Yeah, when no one else is around.

Me: What about at the time it's happening? Do you tell him to stop right now? Or do you ever tell him that you hate the behavior the same way you tell one of the children that you're angry?

(I know she has great parenting skills.)

She: No, I go back and forth between trying to be nice and being scared.

He: If you told me to stop, I would stop.

She: It's a habit to grin and bear it until later. That's usually when I finally get mad. I learned to be nice, especially in front of other people.

Me: It's OK to tell him you're angry when you're angry—especially if you do it the same way you do when you correct children.

He: I really would stop.

She: I'm not really sure I can.

He: I really hate being surprised by you being angry at me when I thought things were OK.

She: OK, I'll try, but sometimes it's really awkward. Like at the block party. I wondered what the neighbors thought when you just followed me to the picnic holding your back while I staggered in carrying the heavy cooler. I just knew they were thinking what a dork you are and wondering why I put up with you.

He: (whining). Well, my back hurt!

She: And you just sat on the cooler the whole time and nobody could even get any drinks out of it.

Me: (to him) What did you tell the neighbors?

He: (defiant) Nothing -- they could see that I was hurting.

She: I don't think so! They really think you're a jerk, and I'm stupid to stay married to you.

Stop Arguing and Start Talking

Me: It really would help if you told people that there was a reason for how you were acting. They don't know your back hurts unless you tell them.

She: It happened at your company picnic, too. When I asked you to hold the play equipment so (their nine-year-old son) wouldn't get hurt, you sort of groaned and said you'd try. When you left, I told your partner that your back was hurting. She told me, "Oh, I just thought he was being a jerk." People really do think you are a jerk!

He: They know I'm very important to the company.

She: Yes, they do but they really feel sorry for me.

Me: What if you both told the truth and talk about what's happening when it happens?

He: (finally getting her point.) OK, I'll try it. I'll tell them when I can't do something because my back hurts.

She: (relieved) I'll try to tell you at the time when you're doing something I hate.

What's Happening Here?

This is just a snippet from an ongoing series of conversations. It lasted only a few minutes.

We've agreed that my job is to help them have effective conversations with each other to improve their relationship. The argument they told me about is a symptom of an underlying pattern that I must help them change.

Each of them is doing things based on old information about the proper way to behave. Each of them hates what the other is doing. Instead of looking at the pattern, they tend to look at each individual incident and argue to justify their own unskilled behaviors.

He learned to expect others to take care of his needs without his needing to do anything to ask for help or to negotiate. When an adult acts that way, he can be perceived as an inappropriate jerk—no matter how smart and important he may be.

She learned that acting angry is forbidden. Since it's almost impossible to never show anger, she saves hers until she can no longer contain it and it spills over in private. By then, it is usually too late to do anything to solve the problem she is upset about.

As they both practice their conversation skills in my office, he is learning about the impact his behavior has on her. He genuinely loves her and is appalled that he has hurt her so often in the past. She is learning that it's far safer to express her small annoyances than she ever imagined it could be, and her angry outbursts are decreasing. Their relationship grows stronger every day.

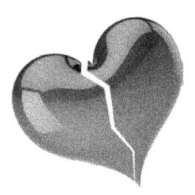

Chapter 16: How to Apologize Even When You Didn't Mean to Cause a Problem

If you've accidentally done something your partner is angry about, you may think you should be forgiven automatically, just because your intentions were good—or at least not malicious. Your partner may disagree.

Just admitting that you have done something is NOT the same thing as apologizing to your partner for your behavior. And just saying "I'm sorry" may not be enough either.

Stop Arguing and Start Talking

After a long conversation, a couple I was working with sorted out the facts about a complicated disagreement. Although they now agreed on the facts, she was still angry with him.

They agreed to let me share this conversation because they hope you can learn from their experience.

The Conversation

She: I want an apology! I have valid information a lot of the time, and I'm angry because you just don't listen to me!

(He says nothing.)

She: Do agree with me?

He: (woodenly) Yes, it's true. I caused the problem because I didn't have the information. You did tell me about it ahead of time. I didn't listen to you. I don't listen about other things, either. I don't read instructions. I don't understand what's going on, and I make mistakes.

She: (very angry) You don't give a rat's ass about what I'm talking about, do you?

Me: (to him) Now she is back to telling you about her resentments. It's because you haven't apologized. You admitted that you caused the problem, but that's not the same thing as apologizing.

He: I told her that I do it in other situations. It happens over and over again.

Me: Do you know what an apology is?

He: I thought I told her I made a mistake and that she's right.

Me: You told her about what was going on in your mind. That isn't an apology. It may be part of an apology. But you've left out anything concerning *her* feelings about the problem you caused. You're only talking about yourself.

Me: (to her). Isn't that why you're still angry?

She: Yeah, he never apologizes.

Me: (to him) (He's looking at the ceiling in exasperation.) Look at me. If this is true for you, repeat it to her. "I'm sorry that you felt embarrassed because of how I acted. If I had listened to what you told me I would have acted differently. I understand why you felt embarrassed by what I did, and I'm sorry I put you in that position."

(Long pause)

He: (thoughtfully and sincerely). I'm sorry about a lot of things about that night. I'm sorry you wound up feeling so badly because of what I did. I'm really sorry I didn't listen, because if I had we wouldn't have had this problem.

Me: (to her). How do you feel now?

She: I feel good. I'm not angry anymore.

Me: (to him) Why was it so difficult for you to decide to say those words aloud?

He: (after another very long pause) I wanted her to tell me she understood my position—that I didn't intend to do anything wrong.

Me: If you know you've caused a problem, you're more likely to get the acknowledgment you want if you tell her that you know and care about how she feels first. After you have apologized by saying, "I'm sorry about the impact my behavior had on you," you can just add, "I did it accidentally. I didn't intend to hurt you."

She: If you did that, I really would be happy to listen to why you did it.

Me: (to him). I think you get into trouble with other people, too, by refusing to apologize because they haven't acknowledged your position. Is that right?

He: (thoughtfully after a very long pause) How can I remember to apologize first?

(He is often thinking when it looks to others like nothing is happening at all. He isn't aware of the effect those long pauses have on other people. I'll talk about that another time. I think he's asked an important question.)

She: I can help with that. If you don't apologize to me, I'll remind you. And you know, it's natural for me to want to understand you after you show me that you understand my feelings.

What's Happening Here?

This conversation is an example of a very common problem.

Resentments are a signal that this situation isn't complete. An apology helps complete an incomplete situation. When resentments come up repeatedly, as they do with many couples, it often means that a heartfelt apology is needed.

A detailed apology must include more than a statement of facts and an admission of wrongdoing. In fact, sometimes it doesn't even need to include either the facts or an admission of guilt.

Sometimes you may not agree that you have done anything wrong. Sometimes the law of unintended consequences is operating, and your good intentions produced an unexpected problem for your partner.

However, even if you're not sorry for what you did, aren't you sorry that your partner is unhappy about the results? That's what you need to apologize for.

The core of an apology needs to include proof (to your partner) that you understand and care about how your partner *feels* about what has happened. Once your partner understands that you really care, your apology may be complete.

Of course, if the problem is something that keeps happening, that probably won't be enough. She or he may insist that the apology is meaningless until you change your behavior.

Resentments tend to disappear once a complete apology is made and accepted. It's kind of like scratching an itch in the right place—the itch goes away.

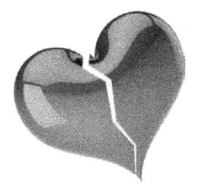

Chapter 17:

What Do You Say When the Answer Is No?

The Risk of Rejection

I found this question posted on my blog.

"Often an individual is very good at identifying his or her needs, wishes and desires and very good at communicating these to a significant other, cleanly and directly, in ways the other person clearly understands.

The other person is also a good listener and communicator and feeds back an understanding of what is being requested, as well as an understanding of how important the issue is to the partner. Thus, communication does not appear to be a problem in the relationship: the message has been sent, received, and fed back accurately.

The problem arises when the answer to the request is a non-negotiable "No," through words, behaviors, or both. Then what happens to communication?

How can people learn to deal with the "risks" of clear communication? How can they develop an appropriate response to "No" that does not discount either of the participants? Is there a "quick and dirty" answer to this question?"

The Quick and Dirty Answer

Sometimes you just can't get what you want.

You may have had the experience of communicating something very clearly to your parents when you were a teenager, and they said no anyway. Their response certainly seemed unreasonable to you then. You probably were angry at them for a while and then you went on with your life.

You may or may not have forgiven them by now. I hope you have. They probably saw a different picture of the world than you did. You may even be grateful now, for their protection back then.

So, the quick and dirty answer is to accept the no, let yourself feel angry for a while, eventually get over it and get on with your life.

The More Complicated Answer

When someone you love refuses your request for something that's important to you, the first thing to do is to assume that she or he has a reason for saying no. You just don't know what the reason is.

If you are both good communicators, the process you described above could be reversed. You can become the listener and ask your partner to elaborate on the reasons he or she has refused the request. Listen respectfully to the answers; they are very important.

When you are certain you understand their side, the resolution may be obvious. If your significant other feels that filling your request would damage him or her in some way, you can both try to figure out if the damage would be real or is simply imagined.

You can also figure out whether the damage to you caused by not having your request met is real or imagined. Once you've figured out both answers, it's time to negotiate.

Sometimes you want something from one person when you could get just as much enjoyment from it from another person altogether. This may or may not be true about your request. If it is true, make an agreement with your spouse that you can get what you want from or with another person.

A good example of a negotiated solution is that my husband never goes to the opera with me. I would like his company, but he hates opera. I either go by myself or with a friend.

Stop Arguing and Start Talking

If this is something you can only get from your partner a nd he or she is completely unwilling to give it to you, you must decide what to do next. It is very important that you consider how important what you want really is to you. It could be important enough for you to choose to leave the relationship.

For example, a woman who wanted children chose to leave a relationship with a man who was not willing to raise children with her.

On the other hand, you may decide that the issue is not important enough to take any drastic action. It's okay to decide to give up something you want in order to have something that you want more.

If this is your decision you may find yourself grieving for what you have given up. That's a healthy and natural response that will run its course.

One of the risks of clear communication is exactly what you said; sometimes you just don't get what you want.

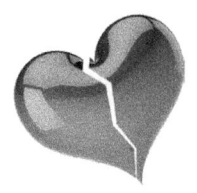

Chapter 18: Conversations Build Happy Relationships

You may think that it takes some magical combination of finding your soulmate and living in a beautiful living situation to have a blissfully happy relationship.

It doesn't!

The real key to experiencing the joy that comes from having an incredible level of connection to your life partner is having the right kind of conversations.

Stop Arguing and Start Talking

In these conversations:

- You share your dreams and talk together about what is important to each of you, even if you disagree.

- You hear each other out without feeling threatened and affirm each other's right to be different and still be together.

- You appreciate how your differences contribute to the richness of your relationship.

- When you encounter problems, you focus on the outcomes you want and how to achieve them, instead of fighting about whose solution is right.

- You are realistic about money and other resources, and you creatively develop the resources to have fun together and achieve your dreams.

You'll create a relationship where:

- You freely admit your vulnerabilities to each other and help each other without depleting yourselves.

- You allow each other the space to be yourselves and willingly risk helping each other grow and change as you evolve both together and separately.

- You create time and space to do what you both love to do while still remembering what drew you together in the first place.

- You create time and space for each of you to do what you love to do alone.

- You love the times you're outrageous and/or silly together.

- When you encounter challenges that seem overwhelming, you find and use outside resources to help you move forward on your life journey together.

- You and your partner empower each other, and the relationship becomes powerful, exciting, playful, nurturing and creative.

- You feel excited, safe and loved.

Idealistic? Certainly. Impossible? Not at all.

If you are going to have a great connection with your partner—you *must* find the time to have the conversations that let both of you feel heard, seen and understood. Less than an hour a week can do the job.

It also helps to understand how normal relationships develop and change over time. By doing this, you don't get upset because your relationship doesn't match the dramatic "soulmate" models that you've been over-exposed to in movies, magazines and popular songs.

You can feel close to your life partner and find the happiness you've dreamed about, instead of giving up because it's gotten hard. Learning the art of having these important conversations makes it easy and fun.

Another book in the Secrets of Happy Relationships Series, *Being Happy Together: What to Do to Keep Love Alive,* has the information you need about relationship development.

It also provides 125 skill-building activities that will teach you to have these important conversations.

Look for samples of several of those skill-building activities at the very end of this book.

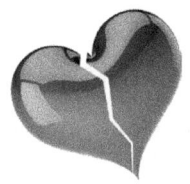

Special Bonus Reminder

If you did not download your copy of *How to Show Respect: Unconditionally* when you started to read this book, do it now.

If you need to know

- What it really means to treat someone you love with respect

- What is probably happening when you think you are doing so but your loved one disagrees
- How to explain why you feel that someone doesn't respect you

Download this brief report to unravel the mystery and create the respectful, happy relationship you really want.

Get it now. www.BooksByLaurie.com/respect

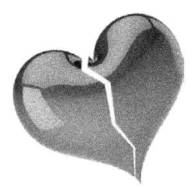

Please Help Me Reach New Readers

Chances are that you checked out the reviews on this book when you purchased it. Reviews are critical to help prospective readers decide to read books. I would be thrilled if you would leave a review NOW, while you are thinking about it.

If you are someone who has done this before, you know how easy it is.

If you're not, you may be shuddering at the memory of grade school book reviews. This is different!!! Really it is!

All you need to do is imagine that you are telling a friend about reading this book. Then follow these steps.

- Say what you would tell your friend into your phone and record it in the notes section and let your phone write it out. (All you need to say is one or two sentences.)
- Email it to yourself.
- Add punctuation if necessary.

Cut and paste your sentences into a review box wherever you buy your books.

I have included a few links to popular places to leave your reviews. Go to www.BooksByLaurie.com or www.Goodreads.com/Laurie_Weiss and click on any book title. Scroll down to find the instructions to leave a review.

I would love to hear from you about how this book impacted you. And, if you have any problems or questions about this book I would really appreciate hearing from you directly. My email address is Laurie@LaurieWeiss.com . You will find my phone number and social media connections on another page.

Thank you in advance for taking the time to contribute to the conversation about what to read. I truly appreciate it.

Laurie

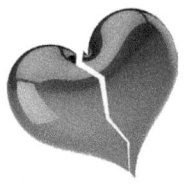

About the Author

Women have been asking Dr. Laurie Weiss questions about relationships for over 45 years. Now she shares her answers to some of them with you.

Relationship Communication Expert, Dr. Laurie Weiss, is internationally known as an expert who helps other relationship consultation professionals develop their skills.

As a psychotherapist, coach, marriage counselor, author and stress-relief expert she has helped more than 60,000 individuals reclaim life energy and find joy in life for more than four decades. She has taught professionals in 13 countries and authored eight books that make complex information accessible to anyone. Her latest, ***Letting It Go***, teaches rapid anxiety and stress relief. http://www.LaurieWeiss.com

Dr. Weiss is one of only two Master Certified Logosynthesis Practitioners in the United States. She is a Certified Transactional Analysis Trainer with Clinical and Organizational Specialties and a Master Certified Coach. Her work has been translated into German, Chinese, Spanish, French and Portuguese.

She is passionate about helping people have the important conversations that build great personal and working relationships. She says, "I have an unshakeable belief, based on over 45 years of experience, that people are doing the very best they can with the resources they have available to them at any given moment."

Dr. Laurie and her husband, Dr. Jonathan B. Weiss, started working together in 1970. Both Drs. Weiss love mixing business and pleasure and enjoy visiting professional colleagues and friends around the globe. They live and work in Littleton, CO, USA.

She loves adventures, went indoor skydiving for the first time at age 67 and zip lining for the first time at age 75. She has been blessed by elephants in India, walked on hot coals, visited Camelot, flown over the Pyramids, and spent an afternoon at the sex temples at Khajiraho and learned more possible sex positions than she can possibly remember.

E-mail: Laurie@LaurieWeiss.com

Office: 303-794-5379

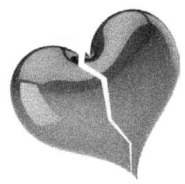

How to Work With Dr. Laurie

My husband, Dr. Jonathan B. Weiss and I have been married since 1960 and business partners since 1972 when we were teaching Transactional Analysis throughout the United States. We have been learning and teaching cutting edge tools for healing and transformation for over 45 years.

We have both been Teaching and Supervising Transactional Analysts for over four decades. Currently we are the only Certified Logosynthesis Practitioners in the United States. Either or both of us would be delighted to help you learn more about creating joy and satisfaction in your life and your important relationships.

Contact Us: We Usually Answer the Phone

You can contact us directly to discuss what is best for you and your group. We offer a variety of options including CLASSES, TALKS, BOOK GROUP VISITS, PROFESSIONAL CONFERENCE PRESENTATIONS, TRAINING, INDIVIDUAL and COUPLES APPOINTMENTS. We work with our clients in person, by phone and by Skype.

Dr. Laurie Weiss:

LaurieWeiss@EmpowermentSystems.com

Dr. Jonathan Weiss: Weiss@EmpowermentSystems.com

Empowerment Systems

506 West Davies Way

Littleton, CO 80120 USA

303-794-5379

Websites

Personal: http://www.LaurieWeiss.com

Logosynthesis: http://www.LogosynthesisColorado.com

Business: http://www.EmpowermentSystems.com

Purchase Books: http://www.BooksbyLaurie.com

Social Media

Facebook: https://www.Facebook.com/laurieweiss

LinkedIn: http://www.Linkedin.com/in/laurieweiss

Pinterest: https://www.Pinterest.com/laurieweiss/

Twitter: https://Twitter.com/@LaurieWeiss

Goodreads: https://www.Goodreads.com/Laurie_Weiss

Blogs

Personal Development:
http://www.IDontNeedTherapy.com/blog

Relationship: http://RelationshipHQ.com/blog/

Business Communication:
http://www.DareToSayIt.com/blog

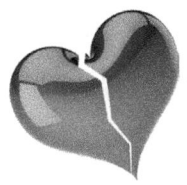

About the Secrets of Happy Relationships Series

Relationships aren't easy. Relationships are often confused and messy with partners trying to find happiness in all the wrong ways.

Real relationships get messy because even though you think your life partner is just like you, he or she isn't. You are two different people trying to meet the challenge of creating and maintaining a happy and loving relationship, perhaps without much useful information.

To make matters worse, you live in the midst of the outmoded role expectations of a culture that values drama and competition and extreme busyness. Most media doesn't help. It focuses on difficult relationships, not successful ones.

Ordinary relationships have their ups and downs and almost nobody writes about those cycles. It's no wonder there are so many misunderstandings. Creating a lasting, loving, growing relationship is an incredible challenge. It's completely natural to have questions about your relationship.

I've been answering questions about relationships since 1973 when I was in newly minted TA (Transactional Analysis) therapist and was sure I had the answers to all the problems of the world. I had been married for 13 years and we had survived some major challenges. I was happily learning and using our new tools. Over four decades later, we are still married, and I've learned a lot.

It's been my pleasure and privilege to help people sort out the misconceptions, misunderstandings and challenges of creating happy, loving relationships. Being happy together is a gift my husband and I have given each other through the work of addressing issues as they arise. It's a gift you can have also; by giving it to each other.

Books in the Secrets of Happy Relationships Series

Are You My Perfect Partner?
To Marry or Not to Marry …
Are you really ready to get married?

Being Married:
Secrets Women Wish They Knew
Crucial information you need
to know about marriage

Stop Poisoning Your Marriage
with These Common Beliefs
Are you letting these myths
undermine your marriage?

Relationship Tips for Life Partners
Critical guidelines for creating a true partnership

Reconnect to Rescue Your Marriage:
Avoid Divorce and Feel Loved Again
What to do before leaving your troubled marriage

Stop Arguing and Start Talking …
even if you are afraid your only answer is divorce!
Are you ready to have these loving,
productive conversations with your spouse?

Being Happy Together:
What to Do to Keep Love Alive
Unlock secrets to rapid relationship
renewal in just an hour a week

Other Books by Laurie Weiss

Letting It Go: Relieve Anxiety and Toxic Stress in Just a Few Minutes Using Only Words (Rapid Relief with Logosynthesis®)
Are you ready for relaxation to replace anxiety in your life?

Emotional Self-Help: I Don't Need Therapy, But Where Do I Turn for Answers?
Do you need to become emotionally literate?
www.BooksByLaurie.com/answers

Recovery From CoDependency: It's Never Too Late To Reclaim Your Childhood
Are you ready to release your codependency?
www.BooksByLaurie.com/recovery

An Action Plan for Your Inner Child:
Parenting Each Other
Are you ready to reclaim your inner child?
https://www.amazon.com/dp/1558741658

What Is the Emperor Wearing?
Truth-Telling in Business Relationships
Do you wish you dared to tell the truth?
www.BooksByLaurie.com/emperor

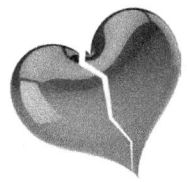

Enjoy this preview of another book in the
Secrets of Happy Relationships series:

Being Happy Together:
What to Do to Keep Love Alive

(Here are 3 of 125 different skill-building activities you'll find in this book.)

Give In--Sometimes

Vary your responses. Don't expect to always give in or to always have it your own way. Getting stuck in any position drains the energy from a relationship.

If one of you usually lets the other have his/her own way in a disagreement, the one who loses will come to resent the situation. The one who wins may be unhappy because it feels like s/he is communicating with a doormat. When you disagree, engage with each other until you actually resolve the issue.

Your weekly assignment, should you choose to accept it:

Look at some of your recent disagreements and see if there's a pattern where one of you is a winner in the other a loser. Choose one recent disagreement and revisit it. Each of you state your own reasons for your position, listen to your partner's reasons and either reaffirm the old decision or make a new one.

Listen, Listen, Listen

Listen carefully to what your partner says. Ask direct questions until you really understand what your partner is telling you. Attentive listening is often the greatest gift you can give another person.

We're often so busy that we barely listen to each other. When we do listen, we're so busy figuring out what we will need to do about what's being said or how we are going to respond, that we listen very selectively.

Your weekly assignment, should you choose to accept it:

Take two twenty-minute time periods where you can practice attentively listening to each other. When your partner is speaking, don't interrupt unless you don't understand what's being said. Ask questions only for clarification and listen to the answers. After your partner finishes speaking, wait at least five seconds before responding.

Do It, Delegate It or Dump It

Hire someone to do the chores you both hate—or do them together. Start by looking at the things that never seem to get done, probably because neither of you wants to do them.

Procrastination is usually a symptom of not wanting to do something. Talk about the symptom instead of ignoring it. Imagine what would really happen if the task was never completed. Then decide what to do. Do not make promises that have been made before.

Your weekly assignment, should you choose to accept it:

List three chores you both hate. Either arrange for one of them to be done by someone else or do one of them together.

***

You'll find links to all the *Secrets of Happy Relationship Series* books at www.BooksbyLaurie.com. Go there now and order the next book you need to create the happy relationship you want and deserve.

www.ingramcontent.com/pod-product-compliance
Lightning Source LLC
Chambersburg PA
CBHW071720020426
42333CB00017B/2345